WALKS FOR ALL AGES
LAKE DISTRICT

© N Leach

WALKS *FOR* *ALL* AGES

LAKE DISTRICT

NORMAN & JUNE BUCKLEY

BRADWELL
BOOKS

Published by Bradwell Books
Unit 1 (Atlantic), Carrwood Road, Chesterfield S41 9QB
Email:info@bradwellbooks.co.uk
© Norman and June Buckley 2014

British Library Cataloguing in Publication Data: a catalogue record for this book is available from the British Library.

1st Edition

ISBN: 9781902674797

Print: CPI Group (UK) Ltd, Croydon CR0 4YY

Design by: Erik Siewko Creative, Derbyshire.
eriksiewko@gmail.com

Photograph Credits: © June Buckley
Except cover image © Shutterstock / Matthew Dixon,
Page 2 © N Leach. Pages 22, 23, 34, 35, 58, & 86 © Shutterstock
Page 59 © National Trust Images / Joe Cornish.

Maps: Contain Ordnance Survey data
© Crown copyright and database right 2014

Ordnance Survey licence number 100039353

The information in this book has been produced in good faith and is intended as a general guide. Bradwell Books and its authors have made all reasonable efforts to ensure that the details are correct at the time of publication. Bradwell Books and the author cannot accept any responsibility for any changes that have taken place subsequent to the book being published. It is the responsibility of individuals undertaking any of the walks listed in this publication to exercise due care and consideration for the health and wellbeing of each other in the party. Particular care should be taken if you are inexperienced. The walks in this book are not especially strenuous but individuals taking part should ensure they are fit and able to complete the walk before setting off.

INTRODUCTION

WHILE MANY OF THE TWENTY WALKS INCLUDED IN THIS BOOK ARE, INEVITABLY, SITUATED IN THE LAKE DISTRICT, ARGUABLY BRITAIN'S MOST COMPACT, DIVERSE AND FAVOURITE WALKING AREA, ALSO OFFERED ARE ROUTES IN LESSER-KNOWN, MORE REMOTE BUT VERY INTERESTING AND ATTRACTIVE PARTS OF THE LARGE AND DIVERSE COUNTY OF CUMBRIA.

The walks themselves, befitting a 'Walks for All' format, are essentially limited to a maximum length of approximately six miles (most are less), do not include mountain peaks or high hill tops, very steep or prolonged slopes, rock scrambling or difficult paths. Stiles are kept to a minimum and the walks are truly for all ages, and for everyone who likes to spend time and get some gentle exercise in fine and interesting countryside. However, access for wheelchairs and pushchairs has not been assessed; there are specialist organisations and publications which cater for these requirements.

The great majority of the walks have public conveniences and refreshment provision. A brief summary at the start of each chapter lists these and other information such as car parking and appropriate maps.

Many walkers will be accompanied by one (or more!) dogs. Some routes are obviously more dog friendly than others. Over many years basic requirements for crossing farmland have not changed. If there is livestock present, the 'on leash' requirement is absolute, often reinforced by notices on gates etc. However, there are many situations where a dog may roam with more freedom, without any risk to other animals or annoyance to people. Experienced dog owners will readily recognise these areas. In this book there are woodlands, lakeshore paths and areas of beach where well-behaved dogs can enjoy considerable freedom.

ASKHAM & LOWTHER

An excellent little walk based on Askham, a village of considerable character. Apart from a little mud, all tracks are good and the aggregate ascent is less than 100 metres.

Askham has two large tree-lined greens and plenty of cottages dating from the 17th and 18th centuries, all blending harmoniously. In addition to the inns there is a post office and general stores.

Askham Hall, in private ownership, is tucked away behind a wall towards the bottom of the village but is to some extent visible from the line of this walk. Founded on a 14th-century fortified pele tower, the Hall was later converted into an Elizabethan mansion, with further re-modelling towards the end of the 17th century. There is limited public access to the gardens and tearoom (see www.askhamhall.co.uk).

Askham's parish church of St Peter, close to the River Lowther, was constructed in 1832 to the design of the architect of nearby Lowther Castle. Despite its Gothic, fortified appearance, Lowther Castle, on the site of an earlier castle, dates only from 1806–11. As the home of the celebrated Lowther family, it was constructed on a huge scale, the north front being 420 feet (130m) long. Unfortunately it was later abandoned for economic reasons and is now nothing more than an elegant but rather sad facade.

Much of the nearby chapel of St Michael dates from the 12th century, probably occupying the site of a much earlier church as evidenced by the 10th-century hogback stones in the porch. There have been many additions and modifications, most notably in the 13th and 17th centuries. Inside are many memorials to the Lowther family and other features such as a gallery formerly reserved for the family and a modern carving in the chancel. The site of this chapel was once within the village of Lowther, demolished by Sir John Lowther in the 17th century and relocated half a mile or so to the east. Beside the chapel is a mausoleum of 1857 with a statue of one of the earls inside.

THE WALK

1. From the church walk downhill to the road bridge across the River Lowther. Turn right immediately after crossing and take either of the two inviting tracks through the attractive mixed woodland; that to the right is recommended as it ascends the valley side at a more gentle gradient than the shorter route to the left.

2. On the more gentle route join a wider track and turn sharply back to the left to rise towards the castle boundary wall. Just after the reunion of the tracks turn right by the angle of the castle wall. Go over a cattle grid to enter a fine expanse of traditional parkland, with the chapel/mausoleum visible away to the left. By the castle gatehouse turn left, go through a farm gate and fork left in 120 yards (100m). The best views of the castle facade are from this area. At the public road turn left and follow the road for less than quarter of a mile (0.5 km) to visit the chapel/mausoleum, returning by the same route.

3. Turn left along a surfaced roadway with a 'public footpath' sign. As the road forks go left, downhill, towards the river where there are two bridges. Low Garden Bridge is a fine old high-arched stone structure, not now safe for vehicles. Beside is a functional utilitarian bridge. Cross either bridge.

THE BASICS

Distance: 3 miles / 5km
Gradient: Some short inclines but mainly level going
Severity: Easy
Approx time to walk: 1½ hours
Stiles: Two
Map: OS Explorer OL5 The English Lakes, North-eastern area
Path description: All on good tracks although one path can be muddy
Start Point: Car park opposite St Peter's Church, Askham, (GR NY 518 239)
Parking: Opposite St Peter's, as above (CA10 2PF)
Dog friendly: On leads for preference
Public Toilets: In local pubs and cafe
Nearest food: Two pubs in Askham. Cafe at Askham Hall (restricted opening in winter)

4. Immediately after crossing turn left, down the bank, to an old iron gate followed by another ascent of the river valley side, this time on a steep, possibly muddy, path through the woods, largely conifer with some rhododendron undergrowth. After levelling out the track continues along the top of the bank, passing fine mature pines and a plantation of spruce.

5. After a little more than half a mile (around 1 km) from the bridge look out for a yellow arrow on a post to the right, just after a rack of fire beaters. Turn right to a ladder stile over a wall and go diagonally across a large field to a stile in the far corner, to the left of an obvious farm gate. There is no path apparent on the ground but there are views of Askham Hall. Over the stile turn left along an unsurfaced lane, passing some of the outbuildings to the Hall, to reach the road in Askham village towards the lower end of the main green.

6. Turn left, passing the Punch Bowl Inn, to return to your car.

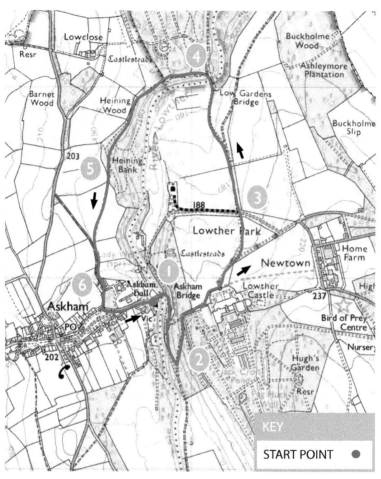

BOWNESS-ON-WINDERMERE

The lake frontage of Bowness is combined with a delightful lakeside footpath in a circuit available to all, with or without boots. No hills, no stiles and plenty of interest along the way.

Bowness has long had the distinction of being the mini holiday town on England's largest lake. The numerous eating and drinking venues, the shops, the lake steamers, launches and sailing boats all contribute to the festive atmosphere.

From Glebe Road, the views to the head of the lake and the mountains beyond are very fine, whilst directly across the water the wooded Claiffe Heights are barely one mile distant. The car ferry operates a timetabled service across the lake from its landing close to the outward limit of this walk.

THE BASICS

Distance: 1½ miles / 2.5km
Gradient: Flat level going
Severity: Easy
Approx time to walk: 45 mins
Stiles: None
Map: OS Explorer OL7 The English Lakes, South-eastern area
Path description: Tarmacked paths and surfaced roads
Start Point: From car park at Rayrigg Road, Bowness (GR SD 403 970)
Parking: Rayrigg Road pay and display (LA23 3DN)
Dog friendly: On leads for preference
Public Toilets: In car park
Nearest food: Huge choice of pubs and cafes in Bowness

1. Leave the car park by the pedestrian exit at the rear of the higher portion. Turn left; this is Fallbarrow Road. In approximately 40 yards (35 metres) fork left along Lowside, passing the Hole in t' Wall Inn. After a short rise turn right, behind St Martin's Church. Pass bollards, then the Old England Hotel, before joining the main street.

2. Turn right to continue along the promenade with the boat landings to the right and the Bellsfield Hotel above to the left. Immediately past the landings turn right, along Glebe Road, with various commercial enterprises on the right and soon with fine views along the lake.

3. As the road bends to the left, fork right at a public footpath with a 'Cockshott Point' signpost, surfaced initially. Go through a kissing gate with a National Trust sign and follow the broad, well-used path towards the lake shore. Cockshott Point is to the right. Between path and lake is a spacious grass area, perfect for family picnics and games. The path stays close to the water as far as a kissing gate.

4. Turn left after the gate (to the right the track leads to the ferry). Go through another kissing gate, passing the Old Rectory before reaching Glebe Road.

5. Go (almost) straight across and follow Rectory Road to rejoin the outward route close to the Tourist Information Centre. Cross the Promenade at the pedestrian traffic lights. Go straight across a road junction and continue along the attractively pedestrianised Ash Street. Go across a mini roundabout to the Albert Inn and along Rayrigg Road, passing below the Beatrix Potter premises, with its fine tea room. Turn left into the car park.

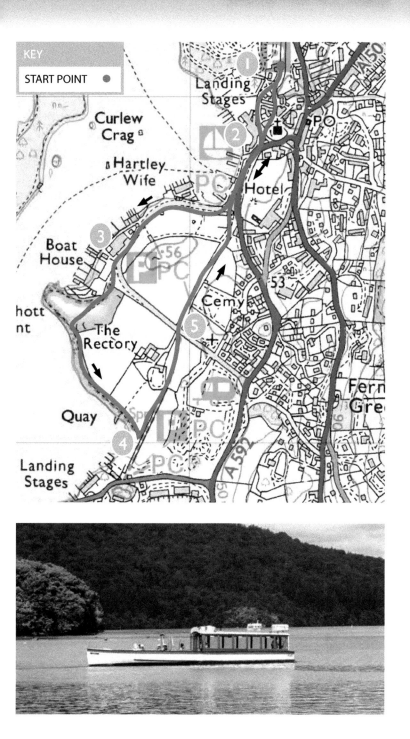

KEY

START POINT ●

Landing Stages

Curlew Crag

Hartley Wife

Hotel

PO

Boat House

Cemy

53

hott nt

The Rectory

Fern Gre

Quay

Landing Stages

BUTTERMERE

A LOVELY, GENERALLY LEVEL, WALK AROUND A BEAUTIFUL
LAKE, WITH GENERALLY GOOD TRACKS AND NO STILES. LESS
THAN A HALF MILE (UNDER 1 KM) ON A MINOR ROAD.

Reached by minor roads from Keswick or Cockermouth, Buttermere sits in a beautiful valley, shared with Crummock Water. On the south-west side of the valley the mountain wall of Red Pike, High Stile and High Crag leads the eye round towards the crags of Haystacks, lower than its neighbours, but the favourite of the legendary Alfred Wainwright and resting place of his ashes. Shapely Fleetwith Pike makes a fine valley head, with the narrow road squeezing along its left flank as the Honister Pass, climbing over into Borrowdale.

Across the valley the smoother slopes of Robinson and Hindscarth are less dramatic but, further north-west, the great bulk of Grassmoor is impressive. After heavy rain Sour Milk Ghyll is a fine sight, plunging over the lip from the Bleaberry Tarn corrie.

Despite its modest size, Buttermere village has an interesting little church (with a Wainwright memorial plaque) and various catering premises; The Fish Inn is renowned as the home of the 'Maid of Buttermere' – Mary Robinson, victim of the imposter 'Colonel Hope'. The story caught the public imagination at the start of the 19th century. Melvyn Bragg's novel of the same name recounts the dramatic events.

THE BASICS

Distance: 4 miles / 6km
Gradient: Mainly level
Severity: Easy
Approx time to walk: 1¾ hrs
Stiles: None
Map: OS Explorer OL4 The English Lakes, North-western area
Path description: Generally good tracks; short distance on a minor road
Start Point: Car park by the Fish Inn, Buttermere (GR NY 174169)
Parking: Pay and display by Fish Inn, Buttermere (CA13 9XA)
Dog friendly: On leads for preference
Public Toilets: In pubs or café in Buttermere
Nearest food: Two pubs and two cafes in Buttermere village

BUTTERMERE

1. From the car park return to the road, bearing right, towards the Honister Pass. In a few yards turn right at a sign reading 'lake shore path'. Go through Syke and Willinsyke Farms to follow a broad stony track descending towards the lake. There is a right turn and a short but comparatively steep section, with rock underfoot, before the lake shore is reached.

2. The path continues through light woodland before reaching a very attractive section where it is squeezed between a steep rocky slop and the water, necessitating a tunnel through the rock. At any junction keep as close to the lake shore as possible.

3. On reaching the Honister road turn right, towards the pass, and continue for approximately one-third of a mile (0.5 km) to reach Gatesgarth Farm, an ancient farmstead with a privately owned car park by the roadside.

PAUSE AND REMEMBER
ALFRED WAINWRIGHT

FELLWALKER, GUIDE BOOK AUTHOR
AND ILLUSTRATOR
WHO LOVED THIS VALLEY.

LIFT YOUR EYES TO HAYSTACKS
HIS FAVOURITE PLACE.

1907 - 1991

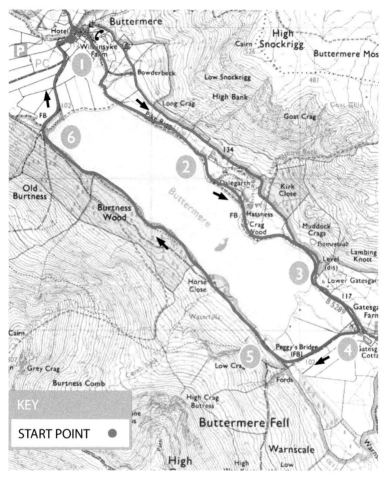

KEY

START POINT ●

4. Cross a bridge over a stream and immediately turn right at a bridleway signposted to Buttermere and Ennerdale. The route through the farm is marked and obvious, heading for the lake shore.

5. Turn right by the far corner of the lake and follow the bridleway to Buttermere, through the National Trust owned Burtness Wood; one section allows a choice between lake shore and a gently rising broader track further up the hillside.

6. At the foot of the lake Sour Milk Ghyll is crossed by a small bridge, followed by a longer bridge over Buttermere Dubs, the lake outflow stream. A broad, easy, track leads back to the village.

CONISTON & YEWDALE

THIS IS AN ATTRACTIVE, EASY, WALK BASED ON THE
VILLAGE OF CONISTON AND VISITING TWO FINE OLD
FARMS, USING PART OF THE CUMBRIA WAY TO RETURN,
WITH SUPERB LAKE AND MOUNTAIN VIEWS. THE BLACK
BULL HAS A LOCALLY ACCLAIMED 'MICRO BREWERY'.

Beautifully situated between lake and mountains, Coniston has a considerable industrial heritage, tourism being a comparatively recent development. The Ruskin Museum, the Ruskin grave in the churchyard and the boating and watersports centre are all worth a visit. The National Trust renovated steam yacht Gondola offers cruises around the lake, whilst the Coniston ferry operates scheduled services to several landing stages, including Ruskin's home, Brantwood, across the lake, which is open to the public in season (www. brantwood.org.uk).

THE WALK

1. From the car park turn left towards the village centre, passing the Crown Hotel, tea rooms and assorted shops. The parish church of St Andrew, mainly Victorian, is by the junction with the main road. Turn right to pass the Black Bull Inn, then left at once into a minor road. Ahead is the impressively steep side of the Yewdale Fells, whilst over the wall to the left Church Beck rushes through the village on its way to the lake. The surfaced road rises steadily as it bends to the right, bordered by rhododendrons and large conifers.

2. Pass Silver Bank, where the road loses its surface and, at the end of a wall on the right, turn sharp right through a waymarked gate. An obvious footpath goes along the

    side of the wall, partly stony, partly grassy, with some mud. Yewdale Fells tower above to the left; to the right longer views include the television relay mast on Claiffe Heights, above Windermere. In about quarter of a mile (0.4 km) turn right at a gate to descend a short, stony track to Far End hamlet. Turn left to follow the surfaced road as far as the main road. At the junction turn left towards Ambleside.

3. In 50 yards (40 m) turn left to leave the road at a gate with a National Trust sign 'footpath to Skelwith Bridge avoiding road' The attractive footpath passes easily through woodland, which has plenty of evidence of former coppicing of the timber. As the woodland thins out, Holme Fell shows up well ahead. Go over two ladder stiles as the path approaches the road.

    (A gate on the right may be used to cross the road and follow the bridleway/access road to Low Yewdale for the shorter walk, which rejoins the main route at point 5).

    Continue along the path and rejoin the road, carrying on towards Ambleside. Pass two road junctions to reach High Yewdale, an old Lakeland farmstead with a hotchpotch of buildings of many generations, including an obvious former cottage in the foreground.

4. Turn right to leave the road at a 'public footpath – Coniston' sign opposite the farm. A level track keeps to the field edge, with a slate on the edge boundary, so common around Hawkshead. Bend right at a kissing gate and go across the next field. To the left, Tarn Hows Wood covers the slope. Low Yewdale is approached by a railway sleeper bridge and kissing gate. Pass straight

THE BASICS

Distance: 4 miles / 6.5km or 3 miles / 5km
Gradient: Modest amount of ascent, without steep gradients
Severity: Easy
Approx time to walk: 1¾ hrs or 1¼ hrs
Stiles: Three
Map: OS Explorer OL6, The English Lakes, South-western area
Path description: Good footpaths, although some may be muddy
Start Point: Car park (GR SD 304975)
Parking: Pay and display in Coniston village (LA21 8EH)
Dog friendly: On leads for preference
Public Toilets: In car park
Nearest food: Pubs and cafes in Coniston

through the farm, reaching an unsurfaced lane with a signpost.

5. Turn left for 'Boon Crag and Tarn Hows'. Cross Yewdale Beck on the bridge and follow the lane as it bends right, rising. In less than quarter of a mile (0.4 km) turn right at a stile/gate to take a just visible path rising invitingly over the grass ahead. As the path becomes a little indistinct, keep straight on to a gate in the wall ahead. Just beyond is a post with a waymark, under an oak tree. The path soon forks at another post with waymark; bear left towards a wall and woodland, still rising.

Shutterstock / Stephen Meese

6. Enter the wood (Back Guard Plantation) at a gate/stile. In the wood, dark with beech, a few foxgloves lighten the gloom. Leave the wood at a kissing gate and then a stile, to enjoy fine elevated views of Coniston village, with the lake and Coniston Old Man soon coming into sight. The path descends initially among gorse to an unusual ruin, with one surviving wall of a once elegant building. Go left through a kissing gate and continue to another gate beside the Yewdale Beck.

Shutterstock / BasPhoto

7. Cross the beck by Shepherds Bridge to reach the public road by the Coniston Primary School. Turn left, then right at a 'T' junction to return towards the village centre and the car park.

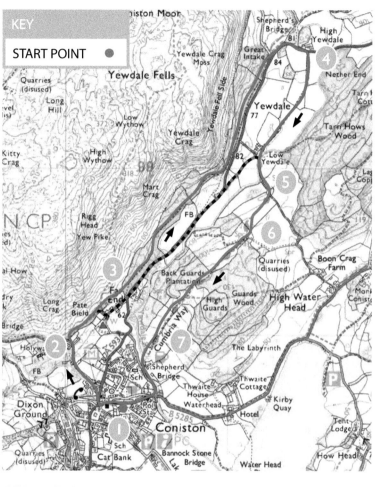

KEY

START POINT ●

Shutterstock / Stephen Meese

ESKDALE TO RAVENGLASS

NOT VERY HIGH AND NOT VERY WIDE, THE THREE-AND-A-HALF-MILE (5.5 KM) LONG MOUND OF MUNCASTER FELL DOMINATES LOWER ESKDALE, WITH THE RIVER ESK TO THE SOUTH AND ESKDALE GREEN AND THE RAILWAY TO THE NORTH.

Between the Fell and the sea, Muncaster Castle (open, with its fine gardens, as a visitor attraction; see www.muncaster.co.uk) has been the home of the Pennington family for 700 years, with close associations with King Henry VI.

The Roman Glannoventa fort lies between castle and sea; the walls of the former bath house are claimed to be the highest above-ground Roman structure remaining in Britain. Ravenglass has one street, leading attractively directly to the sea and sandbanks. The Ravenglass and Eskdale Railway was constructed in the late 19th century at a gauge of three feet to serve mines and quarries further up Eskdale. As trade diminished the railway

became run down; in 1915 it was rebuilt to the present 15-inch gauge as a tourist line. With its attractive rolling stock and well-kept stations it provides a superb return to Eskdale Green. The Barrow to Whitehaven, Workington and Carlisle railway line has a station beside that of the Ravenglass and Eskdale.

This is a linear walk with a return on the delightful Ravenglass and Eskdale Railway (so do look carefully at the timetable before you set out!).

THE WALK

1. Leave Eskdale Green station car park by the approach roadway. Turn sharp right to follow a public bridleway to Muncaster Head and Muncaster Fell. Bear left as the track approaches the railway line and continue between mature trees to a small stream and stile. Go uphill to a large meadow, where the path is ill defined. Keep towards the right-hand edge, heading for a prominent, tree-clad, rocky knoll. After the knoll bear right, along the edge of another meadow, with Muncaster Head Farm below to the left.

2. Join a major track at a signposted junction; turn left, down to the farm, a mixture of traditional stone buildings and modern structures. Beyond the farm turn right and, in 50 yards (50 m), keep right again for Muncaster, rising slightly. A wide, easy track now provides fine walking for one-and-three-quarter miles (3 km) along the foot of the fell, with the broad valley bottom just below to the left.

3. Pass High Eskholme hamlet and follow direction boards, forking left, across a private golf course, then along the edge of the plantation opposite. At the far end

THE BASICS

Distance: 6¼ miles / 10km

Gradient: Mainly on good tracks but with one steep section

Severity: Moderate but with one more strenuous section

Approx time to walk: 3 hours

Stiles: None

Map: OS Explorer OL6 The English Lakes, South-western area

Path description: Good tracks but there is also half a mile by the side of the main road

Start Point: Eskdale Green railway station (GR SD 145999)

Parking: Eskdale Green railway station (Ravenglass & Eskdale Railway)

Dog friendly: On leads for preference

Public Toilets: At the station

Nearest food: Cafe at Ravenglass and Eskdale railway station, Eskdale

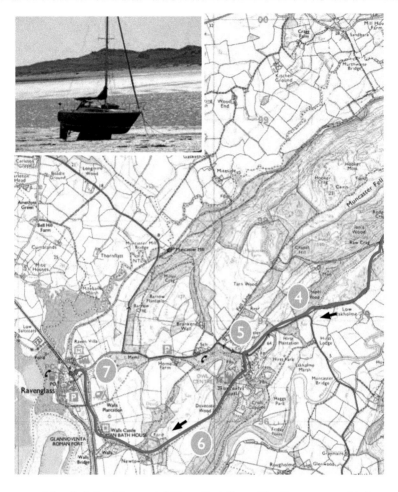

of the plantation take a gate/stile on the left, reaching the access road to Low Eskholme Farm in 400 yards (350 metres). Turn right, cross a surfaced drive, and rise to join the main road.

4. Turn right for a half mile along the roadside, rising steadily.

5. Turn left along an access roadway into the grounds of the castle, signposted as a footpath to Ravenglass. Pass the church, garden centre and cafe. At the ticket office follow the route approved for pedestrians – turn right, then left across the grass between the pond and children's play area. Turn left at the track on the far side and then right, uphill, to follow 'Ravenglass via Newtown'.

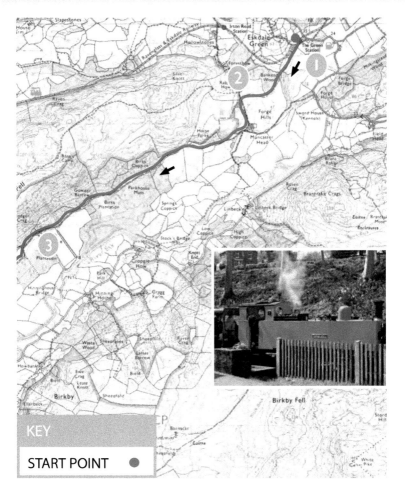

KEY

START POINT ●

6. Leave the castle grounds at a kissing gate. There are now wide views including sea and sand, with the Sellafield nuclear plant prominent. Descend over rough pasture, keeping a little to the right of a knoll, aiming for the middle of a conifer plantation, where a permissive path through the trees leads to the farmstead of Newtown. Turn right at the farm access drive, go straight ahead at a junction and join a surfaced road. Turn right, passing Walls Castle (the Roman bath house). The road continues past a caravan site to join the main road.

7. A little way short of the main road turn left through a gate to follow a footpath to the railway station for the return to Eskdale Green.

GRANGE-OVER-SANDS

Truly a walk for all — largely a stroll along the promenade at Grange, with an optional return by train from Kents Bank.

Apart from one short flight of steps, totally level and good underfoot (boots are not essential), with no stiles or other impediments. Great views across Morecambe Bay.

Grange-over-Sands is a pleasant small town terraced across a hillside overlooking the huge expanse of Morecambe Bay, with wonderful views over the Bay and out to sea. With some of the character of a seaside resort (which it was, in a minor way, many years ago) there is a good range of individual shops, well-maintained public gardens, a promenade and leisure facilities.

The railway has services connecting Barrow-in-Furness with Manchester Airport, calling at Arnside, Lancaster and Preston in one direction and Ulverston in the other. From Kents Bank the train provides a speedy return to Grange unless, of course, a retrace of the outward route is preferred.

THE WALK

1. Facing the railway station bear left to pass under the railway line. Join the promenade, turning right to walk behind the station. The promenade is wide, level and has a hard surface throughout its length. The views are extensive. Behind is Holme Island and the estuary of the River Kent; straight across the wide expanse of Morecambe Bay is the high ground of Arnside Knott; further away is Morecambe itself and the power station

at Heysham Head. The promenade is enhanced by a series of linear gardens, with plenty of attractive seats (note the squirrels!). Between promenade and open water is a wide band of wet, muddy vegetation across which any apparent path is likely to be dangerous. Pass a children's play area, public conveniences and an information board illustrating some of the local wildlife. Next is the seasonal tearoom and a boat-launching ramp. The former public swimming pool is a sad semi-ruin; continue past a 'leisure facilities' signpost, soon passing bowling greens, tennis courts and putting facilities.

THE BASICS

Distance: 2 miles / 3.5km
Gradient: One flight of steps, otherwise level
Severity: Easy
Approx time to walk: 1 hour
Stiles: None
Map: OS Explorer OL7, The English Lakes, South-eastern area
Path description: Pavement all the way
Start Point: Grange-over-Sands railway station (GR SD 412782)
Parking: Grange-over-Sands railway station (LA11 6EH)
Dog friendly: On leads for preference
Public Toilets: At the railway station and in nearby public gardens
Nearest food: Cafe at far end of promenade (seasonal). Pubs and cafes in Grange

2. Bear right to pass under the railway line, reaching a residential area. Turn left in 30 yards (30 m) to walk along the roadside pavement of Cart Lane. Pass a level crossing on the left to follow a 'public footpath Kentsford Road' sign, the path soon becoming narrower but still hard surfaced. Go through two old iron kissing gates and pass  close to the side of a house to reach a flight of steps leading up to another residential road. Turn left along the pavement, descending gently to Kents Bank railway station.

3. Return by train to Grange-over-Sands station.

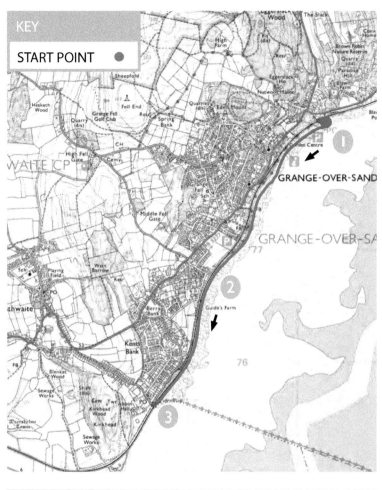

KEY

START POINT ●

HAVERIGG

This is a virtually level circuit linking a remote coastal village with an extensive lagoon encircled by a wide embankment.

Despite having a beach, Haverigg is by no means a typical seaside resort. Formerly a part of industrial Furness, the village has a rather dour appearance. The little harbour is quite attractive and the water-based nature reserve, extending to Hodbarrow Point, is a major feature. During the latter part of the 19th century and the first half of the 20th, this area was subject to extensive and very profitable mining of iron ore, hence the construction of the massive sea wall which provides much of our route. The buildings and other more obvious traces of the once great Hodbarrow Mine have now disappeared.

From this walk there are extensive views across the wide estuary of the Duddon towards Barrow-in-Furness and inland to the gentle hills, outliers of the nearby Lake District.

Surfaced and unsurfaced roadways, excellent paths without stiles contribute to a very easy and straightforward walk.

THE WALK

1. Turn right along the road by the Beach Cafe to reach the side of the harbour. Turn left then right to follow the minor road 'Pepper Hall Walk'. Continue along this narrow, surfaced road to the entrance to Port Haverigg Holiday Village.

2. Fork right, along a path signposted 'public bridleway, Hodbarrow' The path soon

THE BASICS

Distance: 3¾ miles / 6km
Gradient: Level going
Severity: Easy
Approx time to walk: 1½ hrs
Stiles: None
Map: OS Explorer OL6, The English Lakes, South-western area
Path description: Mainly tarmacked paths. A short section of pavement
Start Point: Sea View, Haverigg (GR SD 161784)
Parking: Off Sea View. LA18 4ER
Dog friendly: On leads for preference
Public Toilets: At car park
Nearest food: Beach Cafe and Harbour Hotel

joins an unmade roadway, unmistakably along the top of the old sea wall. Pass a Hodbarrow Nature Reserve board. The lagoon is to the left and the wide expanse of the Duddon estuary is to the right. Pass a trim little lighthouse before reaching a junction in approximately 1¼ miles (2km) from point 2.

Shutterstock © jennyt

3. Fork left at the junction along a lesser track, heading for the remains of a former lighthouse. The path is generally very good; some lengths have been provided with a loose stone surfacing. As the path and a roadway converge, continue along the road before keeping left along a path, close to the water, with a board detailing the water fowl, such as grebe, black-headed and herring gulls, moorhens and mute swans, commonly seen in this area.

4. Follow a 'public bridleway, Steele Green' signpost along a path, with the road close on the right. Join the road, bearing left. Part of the holiday village is to the left. Pass the Commodore bar/restaurant, turning right. The road becomes surfaced before Steele Green hamlet, where 'The Old Gin Mill' is reached. At a 'T' junction turn right, with static caravans of the holiday village to the left. Rejoin the outward route at point 2 to return to the car park.

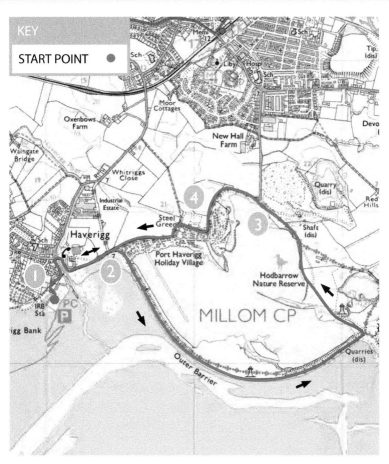

KEY

START POINT ●

Shutterstock © jennyt

HAWKSHEAD

THIS IS A GENTLE RAMBLE IN THE DELIGHTFUL COUNTRYSIDE AROUND. HAWKSHEAD. AS PROBABLY THE MOST PICTURESQUE VILLAGE IN CUMBRIA, FOR MOST VISITORS HAWKSHEAD WILL NEED NO INTRODUCTION.

Particular attractions include the Old Grammar School, attended by William Wordsworth, and the National Trust-owned gallery where a collection of Beatrix Potter's original watercolours, used to illustrate the famous books, is displayed during the summer season (Easter to October).

The parish church of St Michael and All Angels is beautifully situated on its knoll above the village. The earliest portions of the building, including the tower, are more than 700 years old. There were large-scale extensions and renovations around the year 1300 and again around 1500. In addition to the refreshment opportunities there is a good range of other shops.

The Old Courthouse to the north of the village was the gatehouse, the only surviving part of the former Hawkshead Hall, erected by the monks of Furness Abbey as the administrative centre for their varied activities in this part of their widespread domains. The use of the building as a courthouse was in more recent years. It is now owned by the National Trust. There is little to see inside, but a key is available at the National Trust shop in the middle of Hawkshead.

'Ground' as part of a place name, common around Hawkshead, dates from the dissolution of the monasteries around 1540, in this case Furness Abbey, and the division of their estates, creating new farms. The first part of each name is that of the new landowner at that time.

THE WALK

1. Pass the public conveniences, cross Main Street and rise past the front of the Old Grammar School towards the church. Go through the gate and across the churchyard, bearing left to leave the churchyard at a small gate at the top. Note the slate-on-edge field boundaries so typical of this area. Fork right after a kissing gate to follow a public footpath signposted to 'Walker Ground'.

2. Go through two more gates to continue past the Vicarage and the Old Vicarage to a 'T' junction with a rough-surfaced lane. Turn left and then right in 30 yards (25 m) at a kissing gate signposted 'Tarn Hows' etc. Go across the meadow to a kissing gate marked 'Keen Ground only' and then straight across another meadow to another waymarked kissing gate. Views to the right include Latterbarrow with

THE BASICS

Distance: 3½ miles / 5.5km

Gradient: Modest ascents

Severity: Easy/moderate

Approx time to walk: 1¼ hrs

Stiles: Two

Map: OS Explorer OL7, The English Lakes, South-eastern area

Path description: Good footpaths (some may be muddy), unsurfaced lanes and a short length of minor road

Start Point: Hawkshead car park (GR SD 353981)

Parking: Pay and display Hawkshead (LA22 0NT)

Dog friendly: On leads for preference

Public Toilets: In the car park

Nearest food: Several pubs and cafes in Hawkshead

its monument and the higher Fairfield group of fells behind Ambleside.

3. Pass to the right of Keen Ground and go through a gate to join the tree-lined access roadway. Turn right to descend, with Penrose Beck on the left. Turn left at the Hawkshead to Ambleside road, towards the Old Courthouse, now visible. Turn left at the road junction, signposted 'Tarn Hows', passing sawmills with a pond at the rear which suggests the use of water power in former days.

4. Turn right in a further 100 yards (100 m) or so into a surfaced minor road. In a short distance pass Violet Bank and turn right through a gate with a public footpath sign. Cross a meadow to a kissing gate and a stone slab bridge over a stream. The path rising over grass is reasonably distinct, leading to a stile/gate by a muddy section. Pass the prominent house, Fell Field and join a very minor road.

5. Turn right, downhill, with just a glimpse of Esthwaite Water far to the right. Walk to the Hawkshead to Ambleside road and turn left. A permissive path beside the road leads to Outgate and its inn in less than half a mile (under 1 km).

6. Cross the road and take the footpath beside the inn. There is a signpost on the opposite side of the road. Go through two gates in quick succession to follow an obvious grassy track through more waymarked kissing gates. At the corner of a patch of woodland go left over a stile and keep to the path as indicated by an arrow on a post in 100 yards (100 m).

7. On emerging from the wood head for a farm gate/stile and on to a farm, bearing right to reach a public road. Turn left along the road, past the farm, High Loanthwaite, for 100 yards (90 m), then turn right at a kissing gate, signposted 'public footpath, Hawkshead'. The path is well provided with yellow arrows and the village is now set out attractively in front of you. Go along the edge of a meadow, with fine views of the Coniston group of fells to the right.

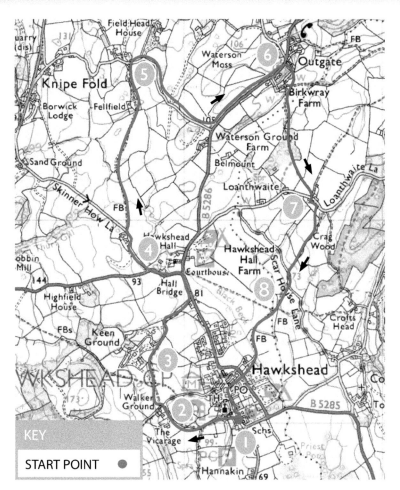

KEY

START POINT ●

8. Join a narrow, bramble-fringed lane (Scar House Lane), turning left. In 50 yards (50 m) turn right at a gate to take a path signposted to Hawkshead. After another stile and a gate, cross a footbridge over a stream, continue towards the village, and turn right to cross Black Beck on a substantial footbridge. A wide track leads up to the road. Turn left to return direct to the car park; go straight across through a waymarked gate for a meander among Hawkshead's attractive buildings.

KESWICK

A LINEAR WALK LARGELY ALONG THE SHORE OF DERWENTWATER, A LAKE OF GREAT BEAUTY. THE RISE THROUGH THE WOODS TO THE LODORE FALLS IS STEADY RATHER THAN STEEP; THE FALLS CAN BE OMITTED IF DESIRED.

Apart from some rough, stony, ground along the lake shore, paths are all good and there are no stiles. Return by boat or bus.

This route includes the celebrated Friars Crag, with the Ruskin memorial stone and a plaque commemorating Canon Rawnsley, co-founder of the National Trust. The lake is seen at its best from the classic Friars Crag viewpoint but there are continuous superb views along the course of this walk. Derwent Isle was the home of the German miners recruited in the 16th century to exploit the mineral resources of the area, St Herbert's Island was reputedly the home of the saint of the same name, whilst Lord's Isle was the site of the house of the Earls of Derwentwater.

The Borrowdale mountains, Maiden Moor, Cat Bells and, to the north, Skiddaw all provide a wonderful setting for the lake, reflected in the water on calm days. The Keswick launches operate a regular service, calling at seven jetties around the lake, alternating clockwise and anti-clockwise sailings, whilst the 'Borrowdale bus' links Seatoller with Keswick.

THE WALK

1. From the car park walk past the theatre to the boat landings, continuing along the roadway towards Friars Crag. Pass the not very prominent plaque commemorating Canon Rawnsley before reaching the Crag.

2. After admiring the view, backtrack a few yards then turn right, along a minor path leading to the John Ruskin memorial stone. Continue along this track, downhill, with a few decrepit steps, to join a more major path. Turn right, following the lake shore

THE BASICS

Distance: 4¼ miles / 7km
Gradient: Level apart from a few steps and one steady rise (which can be omitted)
Severity: Easy/Moderate
Approx time to walk: 1¾ hrs
Stiles: None
Map: OS Explorer OL4, The English Lakes, North-western area
Path description: Mainly good paths but can be uneven along lake shore
Start Point: Lake Road car park, Keswick (GR NY 266229)
Parking: Large pay and display car park on Lake Road (CA12 5DJ)
Dog friendly: On leads for preference
Public Toilets: At car park
Nearest food: Theatre by the Lake and Lodore Hotel

around Strandshag Bay. Continue along the edge of marshy woodland, over a footbridge and through a gate at the far end of the wood.

3. Turn right here, passing Stable Hills and Lord's Island, heading for Calfclose Bay, where the National Trust Centenary Stone (1996) can be seen at the edge of the water. Rampsholme Island is close, St Herbert's Island more distant, with the graceful summit of Cat Bells rising steeply behind. The track and the Borrowdale road are soon close together, tightly squeezed close to the water.

4. Reach the jetty at Ashness Gate; the walk can be shortened by returning from here if desired. Continue along the shore of Barrow Bay, crossing Barrow Beck on a footbridge before reaching Kettlewell car park over another footbridge.

5. Cross the road to take a path into Strutta Wood, signposted 'footpath to Lodore ½ mile'. Some distance along this path, to visit the well-known Lodore Falls take a left fork to rise through the woodland. To omit the falls go ahead to rejoin the road opposite the roadway leading to the Lodore jetty. From the falls take the well-defined path descending steadily towards the back of the Lodore Hotel. Cross the stream on a footbridge and turn left to walk around the rear of the hotel and rejoin the road. The bus stop is less than 100 yards (100 m) to the right.

6. The left turn to the jetty is a little further.

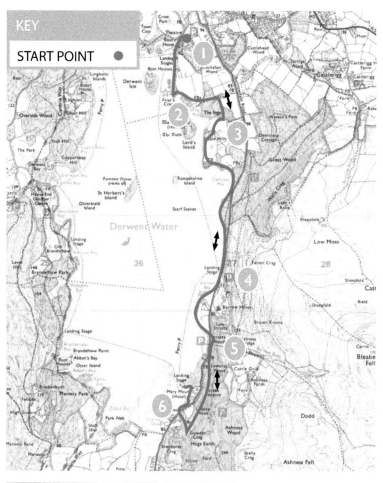

KEY

START POINT ●

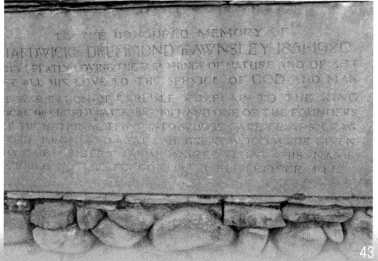

LEVENS PARK

One of the finest 16th-century houses in the north-west, Levens Hall has an Elizabethan appearance despite being founded on an earlier defensive pele tower.

Owned by the Bagot family, it is open to the public during the summer season. Most notable is the garden, with exotic topiary. It has all the usual attributes of a visitor attraction, including a shop and cafe.

Levens Park was initially laid out by Guillaume Beaumont between 1694 and 1710. Bisected by the River Kent, the park is well provided with fine trees, notably the 'Oak Avenue'. There are deer, goats and sheep.

In its short course from the mountains above Staveley to the estuary discharging into Morecambe Bay, the River Kent powered an enormous number of mills of various types in the early stages of the Industrial Revolution. Noteworthy were gunpowder mills providing explosives for the widespread quarrying industry of the Lake District.

THE WALK

1. Walk down to the junction with the more major road (the A6).

2. Immediately before the bridge over the River Kent, turn left to go through a little gate at a 'public footpath Park Head' signpost. There is an information and a 'Welcome to Levens Park' board. The route through the park is over grass, soon rising by the side of the River Kent, excellent underfoot and with views including a minor peak (The Helm, near Oxenholme), seen through the trees ahead. Rise to a gate with a squeezer stile; the main A590 trunk road is now in view. Bear right, keeping close to a wall on the right. Pass another squeezer stile before joining a minor road at Park Head hamlet.

3. Turn right to follow the road; this is a very attractive area, rich in snowdrops in the early months and soon with the river below. At the

THE BASICS

Distance: 3½ miles / 5.5km

Gradient: Level

Severity: Easy

Approx time to walk: 1½ to 2 hours

Stiles: Four squeezer stiles

Map: Explorer OL7, The English Lakes, South-Eastern area

Path description: Easy, level walking on grass, estate paths and canal towpath

Start Point: Layby just north of Levens Hall (GR SD 496853)

Parking: Long layby at the side of the A6 road, a short distance north of the entrance to Levens Hall (LA8 0PD)

Dog friendly: On leads for preference

Public Toilets: At Levens Hall (if open)

Nearest food: Bellingham Buttery at Levens Hall (seasonal opening times)

A590, the track dips to squeeze under the road and above the river. Continue along a cul de sac lane; the river has mini falls and rapids with the apparent remains of a weir and mill pond before a junction with a more important road is reached.

4. Turn right, across the river. Some remains of an early water-powered gunpowder mill can be seen below. At the far side of the bridge go straight across another road to a squeezer stile and a 'Stainton and Canal Towpath' signpost. Rise over grass to a kissing gate, cross a narrow lane, go through another signposted kissing gate and continue to a solidly constructed stone bridge. This is on the line of the Lancaster Canal; under the bridge a section with some water can be seen.

5. Turn right, along a clear path which follows the line of the canal for some distance across a large meadow. Descend to a kissing gate and join a road, bearing left to cross a bridge over the A590. There is a Lancaster Canal Trail signpost close to the near end of the bridge.

6. 100 yards (100 m) after the bridge turn right at a 'footpath to Levens Bridge' sign to re-enter Levens Park through a squeezer stile with gate. There is another of the information/welcome boards. A fine path follows the impressive 'Oak Avenue' through the park. After approximately three-quarters of a mile (1 km) bear right to leave the Oak Avenue, along a delightful riverside track, soon rejoining the A6 road at steps/gate/squeezer stile. Turn right to pass point 2 and return to the parking area.

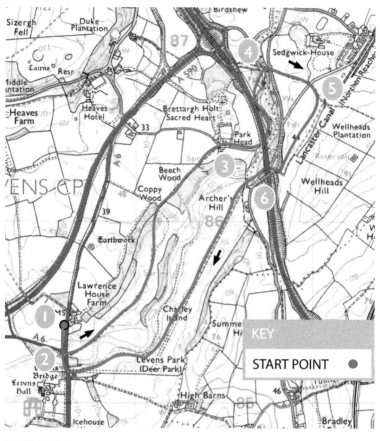

KEY

START POINT ●

LITTLE SALKELD

THIS IS A LARGELY CIRCULAR WALK THROUGH UPLAND
FARMING COUNTRY, WITH SOME WOODLAND. THE
MAGNIFICENT 'LONG MEG AND HER DAUGHTERS' STONE
CIRCLE IS INCLUDED.

The full walk has a little more than a half mile by the side of a quiet road. Otherwise the route is entirely on good footpaths and farm tracks, without stiles. The only significant ascent is the roadside rise from the green in Little Salkeld, steady rather than steep, rising approximately 280 feet (85 m). The reduced walk omits Little Salkeld green and the roadside section.

Little Salkeld is one of the smaller of the numerous villages strung along the course of the delightful River Eden, pretty but without particular distinction. Of greatest interest is the water-powered cornmill immediately below the village, on the road towards Penrith. This renovated mill is open daily, with shop and tea room, selling stone-ground flour and other baking requirements. Tours of the mill are provided three times each day. The adjacent countryside is rather bleak upland farming, including the land occupied by the stone circle.

Long Meg and her Daughters is named in accordance with the not uncommon legend of a woman and her daughters making merry on the Lord's Day and being turned into stone as a merited punishment. There are fifty-nine stones in a great oval of a maximum of 360 feet (110 m) diameter. Some portions of an enclosing stone/earth bank can still be seen.

St Michael's Church, serving the nearby village of Glassonby, has an isolated position at the far end of the route. Pieces of crosses dating from the 9th and 11th centuries can be seen at the church and churchyard. The church replaced an earlier structure swept away by the River Eden.

THE WALK

1. Start along the road leading uphill from the green in Little Salkeld. There is a 'Long Meg Stone Circle. Ancient Monument' sign.

2. Shortly after the prolonged rise eases turn left along an unsurfaced roadway. Go round a right-hand bend, rising gently to join a very minor road. Continue along the road to reach the stone circle. Pass through the circle, staying with the road, past the entrance to a farm. Pass a pond to reach a point where the farm track bends to the left.

THE BASICS

Distance: 3¼ miles / 5.2km or 2 miles / 3km

Gradient: Mainly level, with one short but steady ascent of 280 feet (85 m)

Severity: Easy to moderate

Approx time to walk: 1½ hours to 2 hours (1 hour for shorter walk)

Stiles: One

Map: OS Explorer OL5, The English Lakes, North-Eastern area

Path description: Good paths and farm tracks (longer walk has a short distance on a quiet road)

Start Point: Little Salkeld village green (GR NY 566362)

Parking: Roadside spaces at Little Salkeld green, take the A686 from Penrith towards Alston and turn left at Langwathby (CA10 1NN)

Dog friendly: On leads for preference

Public Toilets: Little Salkeld Mill

Nearest food: Tea room at Little Salkeld Mill

3. On the right is a gate stile with a 'public path' sign. Follow the excellent path, close to the top edge of attractive woodland.

4. The path turns right to a signposted junction. Follow the sign to St Michael's Church, rising gently along a farm roadway, wide and easy. Ignore tracks on the right, continuing to the church.

5. At the far end of the churchyard turn right to head for 'Long Meg, 1 mile', through the churchyard to a gate at the far end. Keep a straight line, over grass, parallel with the woodland on the left. Pass the next signpost, continuing on the same line. There are several little gates and the route is well waymarked. At the edge of a plantation go through another gate, the path now narrower but adequate, slightly downhill. As the stone circle comes into view keep close to the hedge on the left to rejoin the outward route at the rudimentary parking area.

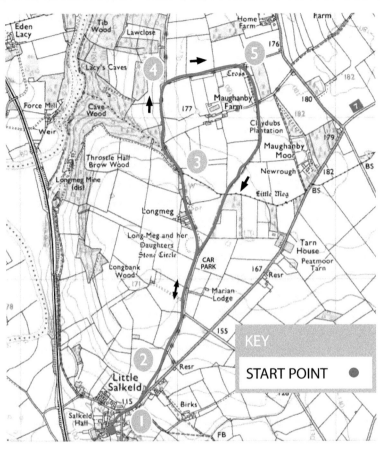

MIREHOUSE

This is an interesting circuit including Mirehouse, the iconic church of St Bega, the former estate saw mill and part of Dodd Wood, with its nesting ospreys.

The tracks are predominantly very good, with ascent limited to approximately 350ft (100 m) and no steep gradients.

Bassenthwaite is the only true 'lake' in the Lake District (i.e. its name is 'Bassenthwaite Lake' rather than a 'mere' or 'water') and this fine circuit gives ample opportunity to admire this splendid sheet of water from vantage points along the lower slopes of Ullock Pike, below Skiddaw. Of enormous interest is the church dedicated to St Bega, standing lonely close to the lake shore, far from any public road. There are legends concerning the ministry of St Bega, daughter of an Irish chieftain, from a 7th-century abbey on this site. Many will no doubt have read Melvyn Bragg's Credo, which builds convincingly on these legends. The present church is certainly of very early origin, probably 10th century, but was extensively restored in 1874. Inside the church there is much to be seen.

The chancel arch is pre-Norman, the transept arch is Norman and the south aisle arch is Early English. The octagonal font is from about 1300 and the wrought iron hourglass holder by the pulpit is of about 1600. The length of sermons was timed, in full view of the congregation, by an hourglass placed in this holder. The Royal Coat of Arms is of King George II, from 1745, the year of Bonnie Prince Charlie, when the congregation perhaps needed to be reminded where their loyalty should lie.

Built originally in 1666 and extended in 1790, Mirehouse has the appearance of a late Georgian manor house. For many years the home of the Spedding family (John Spedding was a school friend of William Wordsworth at Hawkshead), the house was visited on more than one occasion by Tennyson and also by Thomas Carlyle, both friends of the Speddings. Tennyson worked on his 'Morte d'Arthur' here and it is widely believed that St Bega's church close by the lake provided both inspiration and a setting for his famous poem. The house is open to the public in summer, usually on the afternoons of Wednesday, Saturday and Sunday. The gardens are open daily.

THE BASICS

Distance: 3¼ miles / 5km

Gradient: Some slight gradients and a few steps but otherwise level

Severity: Moderate

Approx time to walk: 2 hours

Stiles: Two

Map: OS Explorer OL4, The English Lakes, north-western area

Path description: Good paths

Start Point: Car park on A591 opposite Mirehouse (GR NY 235281)

Parking: Pay and display Forestry Commission car park (CA12 4QE)

Dog friendly: On leads for preference

Public Toilets: At car park

Nearest food: Old Sawmill tearoom (at car park); also at Mirehouse (when open)

MIREHOUSE WALK

1. Walk past the public conveniences to the Old Sawmill tea room. Bear right to the footbridge over Skill Beck, noting the broken dam above which created a pool to provide headwater for the wheel which powered the saws in the mill. Turn sharp left after the bridge, towards the road (blue and yellow waymarks) for a short distance, then go uphill to join a surfaced roadway.

2. Turn right then, in 10 yards (10 m) turn left and go along a good forest track rising steadily (blue waymark), with Ullock Pike above. There are plenty of young conifers, reminding us that the forest here is a commercial enterprise. Glimpses of the lake are soon obtained. Join another track by a rock face and bear left, now level but soon rising again. The path narrows and begins to descend before crossing Sandbeds Gill.

3. Continue downhill, now on a broad track. Keep left at a fork. As the road is approached keep right at a fork, heading for the Ravenstone Hotel, and go straight on as the vehicular track bends sharply to the left. Two stiles close to the road now seem to be redundant.

4. Join the road and turn right, passing the Ravenstone Hotel and Ravenstone Lodge. Turn left immediately after the Lodge. There is a public footpath signpost tucked away in the hedge and there are three steps down from the road. After a gate/stile and some huge conifers, cross a meadow on a lightly used path to a kissing gate.

   Lord's Seat and Broom Fell are the hills straight ahead, on the far side of the lake. There is a curiously stepped land form in the next field. Walk along the step towards a group of trees and bear left to a tiny stream and a stile over a fence. Continue along the now obvious path among well-spaced oak trees. Go through several more kissing gates to a rather incongruous electricity substation.

5. Cross a minor road to a gate/stile with a 'St Bega's church' notice. Follow the farm track. Dodd is the conical hill showing well above the wood and the car park of the

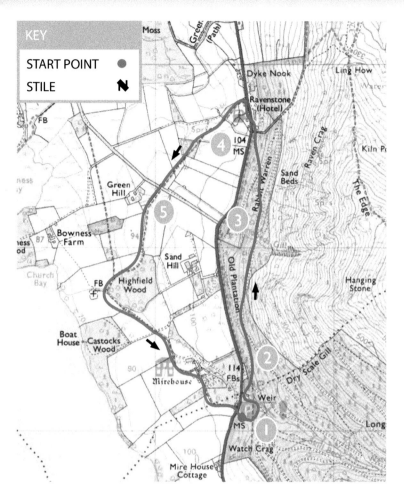

same name. The farmstead to the left is Sand Hill. A gentle descent along the edge of Highfield Wood leads directly to the church and a modern cross with mounting block marking the site of occasional open-air services. After perusal of the church and its surroundings, retrace footsteps for 50 yards (50 m) and turn right immediately before the stream to follow a narrow path beside the stream and by a line of great oaks towards Mirehouse. Go through metal gates and keep to the designated footpath through the grounds. Turn right by outbuildings to follow a gravelled driveway, reaching the public road by a gate to the right of a roadside house. Turn left for 50 yards (50 m) and cross the road to the entrance to the car park and the Old Sawmill tea room.

NEAR & FAR SAWREY

Moss Eccles Tarn is a most attractively situated small lake easily reached from either Near or Far Sawrey.

The walk described here, from Far Sawrey to the tarn, returning via Near Sawrey, is particularly appropriate for a fine day, with the option of a tarnside picnic.

Near and Far Sawrey are attractive small villages along the road from Hawkshead to the Windermere ferry. The former has the world famous Hill Top, Beatrix Potter's former home, long owned by the National Trust and open to visitors from Easter to October. There is also the Tower Bank Arms, a rare example of an inn owned by the National Trust.

THE BASICS

Distance: 3 miles / 5km

Gradient: Mainly level with minimal ascent

Severity: Easy

Approx time to walk: 1 hour

Stiles: None

Map: OS Explorer OL7, The English Lakes, South-eastern area

Path description: Broad, easy tracks

Start Point: Far Sawrey village (on B5285 between Hawkshead & Windermere ferry) (GR SD 379954)

Parking: Small car park at Village Institute, Far Sawrey, almost opposite the Cuckoo Brow Inn

Dog friendly: On leads for preference

Public Toilets: None

Nearest food: Cuckoo Brow Inn, Far Sawrey or Tower Bank Arms, Near Sawrey

1. Walk down the road past the inn, forking right in 100 yards (100 m) to follow a sign 'public bridleway to Moss Eccles Tarn and Claiffe Heights'. The surfaced roadway rises, passing the Old Vicarage, with views to the left over Near Sawrey village to the Coniston group of fells. Go through a kissing gate to head for Righting, an impressive house ahead. Fork left to leave the drive at a 'Hawkshead' sign. The good broad track crosses Wilfin Beck on a footbridge, rising again to join the similar track from Near Sawrey.

© Shutterstock/David Hughes

2. Bear right, past a 'bridleway, Claiffe Heights' sign, rising again. After a gate there is an area of great rocky slabs before Moss Eccles Tarn is reached. This was a favourite place for Beatrix Potter who for many years kept a rowing boat on the tarn.

3. Turn round and return to the fork. Continue along the broad track to the right descending to Near Sawrey, for Hill Top and the Tower Bank Arms.

4. Join the road in Near Sawrey, turning left to pass the entrance to Hill Top. In about 200 yards (200 m) look for a signposted 'footpath to Far Sawrey' on the right, staying close to the road, to return to Far Sawrey and the car park.

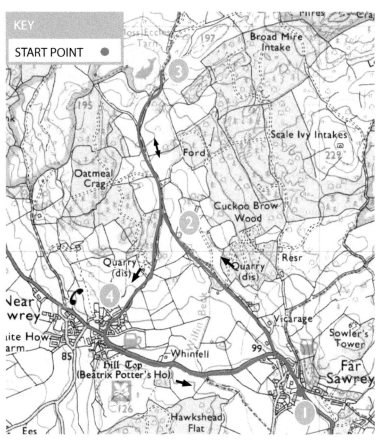

KEY

START POINT ●

© National Trust Images Joe Cornish

POOLEY BRIDGE

THIS WALK IS A CIRCUIT LINKING POOLEY BRIDGE AT THE FOOT OF ULLSWATER WITH DACRE VILLAGE AND WITH DALEMAIN, AN ELEGANT STATELY HOME.

To the north-east of the rough, craggy, area of central Lakeland, the nature of which is determined by the rocks of the Borrowdale volcanic series, this is a landscape of more gentle rolling hills. Much younger sandstone and limestone are the geological base on which this attractive countryside is founded. Pooley Bridge is only a modest settlement by the foot of Dunmallard Hill, but it is provided with inns, tea rooms, shops, an information centre, public conveniences and car parks. It is also the terminus of the 'steamer' service from Glenridding, at the other end of the lake.

Dacre is a quiet, attractive, little village, with an inn and two important features. Firstly, St Andrew's Church is claimed, on evidence from the Venerable Bede, to be on the site of an Anglo-Saxon monastery. The present structure was extended in the 13th and 14th centuries and then considerably restored, including rebuilding of the tower, in the 19th century. Inside, there is a fragment of a carved 9th-century Anglian cross in a window and a 10th-century stone of the Viking period on the floor. The large lock of the south door is dated 1671 and is inscribed A. P. – Anne, Countess of Pembroke, better known as the legendary Lady Anne Clifford, whose steward Sir Edward Hasell later lived at nearby Dalemain.

In the churchyard are the famous Dacre bears (and cats/lynxes?) – four greatly eroded carved stone creatures by the corners of the original churchyard. Dacre's second main feature is the castle, a 14th-century pele tower designed to resist marauding Scots, on

the site of an older fortification. Used as a private residence, the castle is not open to the public, but the footpath passes sufficiently close to allow a good view.

The estate of Dalemain was purchased by Sir Edward Hasell in 1680 and is still owned by the same family. Most of the present Georgian structure – the East Front and the sides – dates from 1740–50, but the west range is much earlier, of the 15th and 16th centuries. During the season (broadly from early April to early October) the house and gardens and small museum are open to the public as a visitor attraction. Accessible without charge are a gift shop and tea room.

THE WALK

1. Set off along the broad track at the far end of the Dunmallard car park in Pooley Bridge, an inviting route close by the side of the River Eamont, below the wooded side of Dunmallard Hill. Go through a little gate and across the foot of a meadow. As a fence is approached fork left to rise along a barely defined path which soon turns sharply towards the fence, reached at a gate and stile.

2. Go over the stile and turn left. Keep close to the fence for quarter of a mile (0.5 km) on a slightly vague footpath. The Helvellyn group of mountains comes into view to the far left as the shapely mound of nearby Dunmallard Hill is passed. The Penrith

THE BASICS

Distance: 5¾ miles / 9.2km

Gradient: No steep gradients; some gradual ascents

Severity: Moderate

Approx time to walk: 2½ hours

Stiles: Four

Map: OS Explorer OL5, The English Lakes, North-eastern area

Path description: Farm tracks, minor roadway and grassy footpaths underfoot, plus about a quarter of a mile along the verge of the A592

Start Point: Dunmallard car park, Pooley Bridge (GR NY 469244)

Parking: Dunmallard P&D car park across the bridge from Pooley Bridge village (CA11 0LL)

Dog friendly: On leads for preference

Public Toilets: In Pooley Bridge

Nearest food: Inns and tea rooms at Pooley Bridge. Tea room at Dalemain

road is reached at a farm gate/stile. Go straight across to a kissing gate and 'public bridleway' sign. The track is again a little faint on the ground, but keep the fence close on the left. Place Fell, by the head of Ullswater, is now in view as the way rises towards a very minor road, passing a few huge trees on the field boundary. By the roadside, just to the left, is the first of several iron seats in the Dacre area which commemorate the coronation in 1953.

3. Turn right at the road and then left at a junction in less than a quarter of a mile (0.5 km), at a 'Dacre ½m' signpost. After an initial slight rise, the road descends steeply to Low Bridge, crossing Dacre Beck. Wide verges make for good walking and there are soon views through the trees to Dacre Church and the nearby castle. Close to a house entrance drive look out for an old boundary stone on the left, separating the ancient townships of Dacre and Soulby. In the bottom, before the bridge, is the Lord's Waste access area. Cross the bridge and rise through the village towards the inn and the church.

4. After seeking out the bears in the churchyard, return as far as the mini village green, which has a stone pillar with attachments, presumably a relic of the village stocks.

5. A roadside signpost on the left (as approached from the church) points to two public footpaths, both through a farm gate. Go through the gate, staying with the main track, bearing right to pass close to Dacre Castle. The farm track continues unmistakably, generally straight and level, towards Dalemain. On a clear day the view ahead includes part of the distant Pennine Hills, on the far side of the Eden Valley. The Dalemain estate is entered beside a row of trees, with the stately house visible across the fields. A slight rise through woodland leads directly to the courtyard behind the house, with tea rooms and gift shop.

6. After any visit to the house, gardens, museum, gift shop, or for refreshments, exit from the courtyard under the arch, heading for the car park. Turn right by the car park, and then bear left towards the main road. Turn right at the road to walk to the bridge over Dacre Beck. About 60 yards (50 m) to the right is a much older bridge, presumably the original road bridge. Very obvious in this part of the Lake District is the sandstone which has, in addition to its fundamental contribution to the landscape, provided plentiful building material.

7. Turn right immediately after crossing the bridge, over a stile. The correct line is now to head for the near end of the old bridge, then turn left to aim for the left edge of Langfield Wood, nearly half a mile (1 km) ahead across the huge rising field. Until fairly close to the wood, the path is not well defined on the grass. After passing the

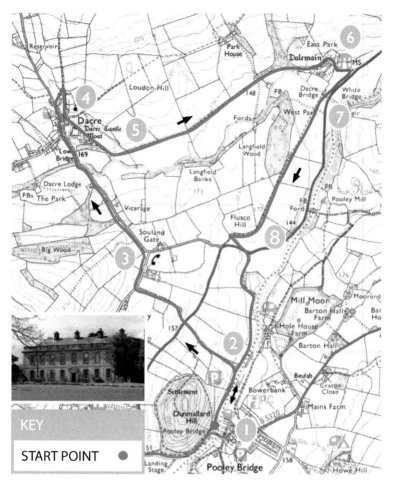

KEY

START POINT ●

end of the woodland, the route becomes well marked, with fine views to Dunmallard Hill and the Helvellyn group of fells. As the main road is approached, bend right and descend to the road through a gate and over a stile.

8. Turn left along the roadside for approximately 100 yards (100 m) and, as the road bends to the left, turn right at a signposted kissing gate. The likely mud on this section is largely avoided on walkways. Go left at a gate/stile, then to the right of an artificial pond, turning right at a kissing gate to reach the wooded bank of the River Eamont, along which an altogether gentle and attractive path heads straight back to the car park, rejoining the outward route on the way.

ROSTHWAITE & SEATOLLER

THIS IS A FINE CIRCUIT WHICH HAS, IN MINIATURE, MOST OF THE ESSENTIAL FEATURES OF A LAKE DISTRICT WALK: A SHARP LITTLE PEAK, SOME STEEP ASCENTS AND DESCENTS ON STONY PATHS, WOODLAND, A GENTLE RAMBLE BY THE SIDE OF A LOVELY RIVER AND TWO ATTRACTIVE SETTLEMENTS.

For many, Borrowdale is the finest of Lakeland's numerous valleys. Its considerable length and rich variety of landscape, including the traditional buildings of the small villages and hamlets, and its penetration to the heart of the great central mountains make an unbeatable combination. In particular, the wide area of green fields above the famous 'Jaws of Borrowdale', generous by Lakeland agricultural standards, is cut off by the constriction and it is easy to appreciate its former isolation, the consequent insularity of its people, and the 'Kings of Borrowdale' title applied to their leaders centuries ago. Centre of this delectable area is Rosthwaite, with two inns and the 'Flock In' tea shop supplementing its basic farming activity. Seatoller is another attractive settlement a little further up the valley, at the point where the road makes its escape by the steep and high climb to the Honister Pass and on to Buttermere.

Castle Crag is a remarkable little peak, at about 985 feet (290 m) the only summit of less than 1,000 feet to appear in the late A. Wainwright's classic mountain guides. What a distinction; earned, no doubt, by the sharpness of the peak and the uncompromising steepness on all sides, as the Crag stands well clear of the bulky fell of which it really an offshoot. The woodland on the slopes adds to the attraction and hides most of the extensive

quarrying which left many scars and holes. The side of the Crag overlooking the river has caves which, early in the 20th century, were inhabited in summer by a well-known eccentric, Millican Dalton.

THE WALK

1. Walk to the road and turn right to pass through the tiny village of Seatoller (note the plaque on the wall by the roadside). As is obvious from the gradient, this is the start of the Honister Pass. Hause Gill tumbles noisily to the left, with a charming little bridge. Ignore a kissing gate on the right. As the road bends to the left, turn right to climb the roadside bank, up to a gate.4. Cross a gill on a footbridge and enjoy the view of the former 'kingdom' of upper Borrowdale below. Rosthwaite is soon visible. Cross another bridge and continue to the junction where the path from Dale Head via Rigghead Quarries joins on the left.

2. Go up the steep hillside on a well-marked path, engineered in part, through the bracken. To the left is Seatoller Fell, below Grey Knotts; behind is the great bulk of Glaramara. Keep left at a fork and rise to join a broad, stony, track. Turn left for a short distance, facing up towards the Honister Pass.

3. At a cairn with a discreet little signpost fork right towards 'Grange'. Rise over grass to a gate in a wall and turn right along a path on the far side of the wall. The ascent soon comes to an end. This well-used path is part of the designated 'Allerdale Ramble'. The path passes behind the minor hill, High Doat. Ahead, Castle Crag and King's How are soon in view.

THE BASICS

Distance: 4 miles / 6.5km or 3 miles / 5km
Gradient: Some steep ascents and descents on stony paths
Severity: Moderate: some steep sections
Approx time to walk: 1 ½ hours
Stiles: Three
Map: OS Explorer OL4, The English Lakes, North-western area
Path description: Good paths, stony in places, but with an awkward section near the youth hostel
Start Point: National Trust car park at Seatoller on B5289 (GR NY 245138)
Parking: National Trust car park at Seatoller (CA12 5XN)
Dog friendly: On leads for preference
Public Toilets: At the car park
Nearest food: Inns and cafes at Rosthwaite. Cafes at Rosthwaite, Seatoller and the youth hostel

4. Cross a gill on a footbridge and enjoy the view of the former 'kingdom' of upper Borrowdale below. Rosthwaite is soon visible. Cross another bridge and continue to the junction where the path from Dale Head via Rigghead Quarries joins on the left. (Turn right here and descend to New Bridge for the shorter version of the walk, omitting Castle Crag.)

5. The full walk continues by crossing Tongue Gill on two footbridges, followed by a stony section of path. Across Borrowdale the Langstrath Valley joins the main valley below Stonethwaite hamlet. Behind Stonethwaite is the abrupt and soaring Eagle Crag. As the path starts its descent, the views of Derwentwater and Skiddaw to the north are a sample of what can be seen from the summit of Castle Crag.

6. In a short distance, downhill, look for a right turn and a path leading up to a stile over a wall. The precipices of the Crag look formidable but fear not, there is a perfectly safe way to the top. On the right is a seat with a plaque to Sit William Hamer, who gave this land to the nation in 1939.

7. Go over a ladder stile and an ordinary stile and continue along the obvious path, soon reaching a junction. For the top go left and tackle the enormous quarry spoil heap, then bear left above the rim of the summit quarry. The views include Skiddaw and Blencathra to the north, Helvellyn to the east, and an array of fells to the south, including Scafell Pike, Scafell and Great Gable. Descend back to the junction and turn left to a ladder stile. (To omit the summit turn right at the junction to go direct to the ladder stile.)

8. After the stile the path descends quite steeply, over grass initially, to a gate in a wall. Enter woodland to continue the steep descent to the valley bottom path, joined at a gate/stile. Turn right to follow this broad, easy, route to Rosthwaite, crossing the River Derwent at New Bridge or, for the more adventurous, by the stepping stones 300 yards (250 m) or so upstream. The teashop is on the left, opposite Yew Tree Farm. Note the weather vane on the roof.

9. Leave the teashop and take the surfaced roadway to the left of Yew Tree Farm, passing some fine traditional cottages. In approximately 100 yards (90 m) turn right to leave the lane immediately before the house named 'Stone Croft'. In 25 yards (20 m) turn left through a gate, signposted 'Path to Longthwaite Y.H.A.'. Go along the edge of the field to a waymarked stile and then diagonally right to a gate with a huge boulder built into the adjacent wall. Bear left to Peat Howe hamlet. Note the slate-on-edge boundary to the left, rare except in the Hawkshead area.

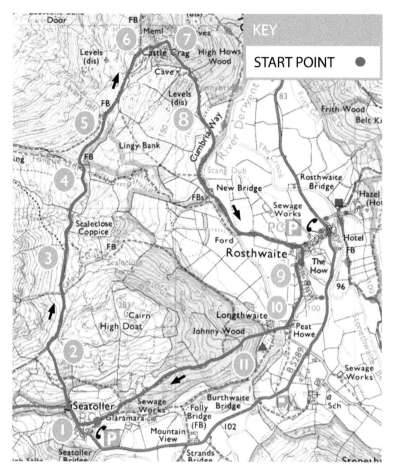

KEY

START POINT ●

10. Turn right along the surfaced roadway, cross the bridge over the river, and bear left to pass across the front of the youth hostel/cafe. After a kissing gate there is a short scrambly section (70 yards (65 m) or so) by the side of the river. Take reasonable care and there is no real danger. At this point the river is progressively cutting away the end of a long glacial moraine, revealing the composition of the debris piled up by the moving ice a few thousand years ago.

11. The path continues by a wall along the lower edge of Johnny Wood, maintained, like so much of Borrowdale, by the National Trust. As a large holiday centre building is approached, go right, up to a gate in a wall then bear left. Seatoller is soon in view, the path going through a gate/stile direct into the car park.

RYDAL

INCLUDING TWO OF LAKELAND'S BEST-LOVED FOOTPATHS, THIS WALK HAS MOST OF THE ATTRIBUTES WHICH MAKE WALKING IN THE DISTRICT SO SPECIAL.

Lake, river and mountain views combine to produce a circuit of spectacular beauty, with the added interest of the Rydal caves. Underfoot, the paths are first class throughout. There are no severe gradients and no stiles.

Apart from its undisputed beauty, the Rydal (Rye Dale – the valley where rye is grown) area has a great deal of interest for the visitor. Rydal Hall was for more than 300 years the seat of the Le Fleming family. In modern times it was purchased by the Diocese of Carlisle and is now used as a conference centre and retreat, with camping site and youth centre in the grounds. The present structure is largely of the 17th century, with a late 18th-century facade.

Rydal Mount was the home of William Wordsworth from 1813 until his death in 1850. The house is an 18th-century enlargement of a much earlier farmhouse and is open to the public all the year round, apart from a midwinter break of a few weeks. The

furnishing is much as it was in Wordsworth's time, including family portraits and chair seats embroidered by Mary and Dorothy Wordsworth and Sara Hutchinson. The large garden is attractive, with terraces created by Wordsworth himself and some splendid long views.

Rydal Church was originally a chapel, built by Lady le Fleming in 1832 at a cost of £1,500. It was enlarged in 1884. Externally the building is unremarkable, but inside the pews occupied by Wordsworth, who was a chapel warden, and Dr Arnold (of Rugby School fame) can both be identified. The balcony, with its separate entrance, was reserved for the le Fleming family. Various plaques and windows commemorate members of these families.

Behind the church is Dora's field, with great banks of daffodils. Wordsworth purchased the field in 1826 when eviction from Rydal Mount by his landlady, Diana le Fleming, seemed likely. He did some work on the design of a house for the site but, when eviction was no longer a threat, he gave the field to his daughter Dora. The celebrated poem has nothing whatsoever to do with these daffodils!

* Areas for parking on both sides of the A591 Ambleside to Grasmere road. There is also a frequent bus service to White Moss Common (555 and 599 routes from Kendal/Windermere and Ambleside/Grasmere/Keswick).

THE BASICS

Distance: 3 miles / 5km

Gradient: No severe gradients

Severity: Easy

Approx time to walk: 2 hours

Stiles: None

Map: OS Explorer OL7, The English Lakes, South-eastern area (1:25,000) or Landranger 90, Penrith and Keswick (1:50,000)

Path description: First-class paths

Start Point: White Moss Common car park (lower side) (GR NY 350065)

Parking: Pay and display car park at White Moss Common (LA22 9SE)*

Dog friendly: On leads for preference

Public Toilets: At the car park

Nearest food: Tea rooms at Rydal Mount and behind Rydal Hall

1. Cross the road if parked in the old quarry part of the car park and, from either part, pass the public conveniences and take the broad track close to the side of the River Rothay.

2. Cross the footbridge over the river. The way to Rydal Water (and Loughrigg Terrace) is straight ahead through White Moss Wood as indicated on the signpost. The very well-used track rises easily among the trees to reach a gate in the top wall.

3. Go through and turn left. There are two good paths to Rydal, the one descending by the side of the wall being slightly the shorter. The upper path is recommended for superior views and for a visit to the Rydal caves. This path rises a little at first as it crosses part of the flank of Loughrigg, then maintains its height above Rydal Water. The views are marvellous; across the lake is the Fairfield group of mountains, ending abruptly with Nab Scar, towering above Rydal. Helm Crag is visible towards Grasmere and the lake itself has a most beautiful setting. Go over a rocky nobble to reach a former quarrying area, which includes the massive Rydal cave, ahead.

4. From the cave go steeply downhill, passing the lower cave, accessible only to those prepared to climb an awkward little rock face. At a gate by the near end of woodland, zig-zag left and right to descend to the lake shore. Go through a kissing gate into the Rydal Woods Access Area. Leave the wood by a similar gate and follow the path to a footbridge over the River Rothay. Rise to the main road and turn right for about 130 yards (120 m).

5. Turn left up the cul de sac road leading to Rydal Mount. On the left is Rydal church, with Dora's field behind. A little further is Rydal Hall (turn right at the second vehiclar entrance to walk to the tea shop in less than 150 yards (150 m)). This roadway is the only right of way through the grounds of the Hall, but entrance to view the formal gardens, laid out by Thomas Mawson early in the twentieth century, is usually permitted. Rydal Lower Fall, with viewing house, can also be visited. From the tea shop return to the road and turn right, rising steeply to pass Rydal Mount.

6. Turn left at a 'coffin route to Grasmere' sign to take the old 'corpse' or 'coffin' road. Go through a gate and continue along the excellent track which rises and falls across the lower slopes of Nab Scar. Wansfell Pike is dominant in the view behind. Apart from the odd stony section, the track is easy.

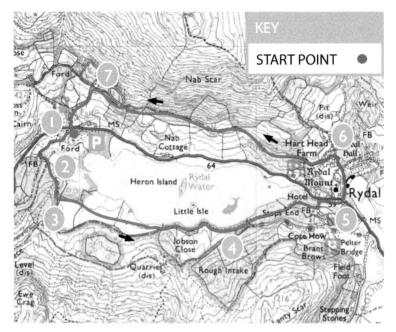

7. Thirty-five yards (30 m) after a gate turn left down a steep path between widely spaced walls. There is abundant bramble and the accompaniment of a rushing little stream beside the track. Near the bottom the stream joins a bigger stream, with a waterfall. At the main road turn left to return to the lower car park, or right to return to the old quarry car park.

KENDAL: SCOUT SCAR

A FAVOURITE WALK WITH LOCALS; AFTER THE INITIAL SHORT ASCENT THE TOP OF SCOUT SCAR OFFERS THE EASIEST POSSIBLE STROLL AND THE DISTANCE WALKED CAN BE VARIED. THE VIEWS ARE SUPERB.

TScout Scar is a broad ridge, two miles (3 km) long, situated to the south-west of Kendal. It is a surviving part of the limestone which formerly covered the other various Lake District rocks. The west side of the scar is precipitous, with more gentle slopes on the east side. The views from this modest height (a little more than 700 feet or 200 metres) are very wide ranging – Lake District mountains to the north and west and the Pennines to the east.

There is also botanical interest, with a range of lime-loving plants which are largely absent from the Lake District and are, in some cases, at the north-western limit of their range.

THE WALK

1. Cross the road to a gate opposite the car park. Follow the well-worn track, rising quite steeply for approximately 35 yards (30 m). Having reached the top of the scar, several paths are apparent, all heading in much the same direction. Walkers may wander at will; the recommended route is to keep close to the top of the cliff face on the right, with the

finest views of the meadows of the Lyth valley below and the more distant Lakeland mountains. Ahead is the estuary of the River Kent, part of Morecambe Bay, with the hill of Arnside Knott beyond. The distance walked is optional. For a circuit of two-and-a-quarter miles (3.5 km) continue until opposite and above the large farm of Barrowfield.

THE BASICS

Distance: 1mile / 1.5km or 3 miles / 5km

Gradient: Initial short ascent then an easy stroll

Severity: Moderate; initial steep ascent

Approx time to walk: 30 minutes or 2 hours

Stiles: None

Map: OS Explorer OL7, The English Lakes, South-Eastern area

Path description: Good quality, dry underfoot

Start Point: Car park on the Kendal to Underbarrow road (GR SD 493926)

Parking: Car park close to the summit of the Kendal to Underbarrow road, (LA8 8HA). From Kendal town centre follow the Underbarrow road, rising for approximately two miles / 3 km

Dog friendly: On leads for preference

Public Toilets: Nearest are in Kendal town centre

Nearest food: None on the route; plenty of choice in Kendal town centre

2. Turn left at a large stone cairn, rise to the top of the ridge, then turn left again, heading towards the trig point at the summit. Ingleborough and the Howgill Fells above Sedburgh are now particularly well seen. From the trig point the path continues to the prominent shelter building. From the building the route rejoins the outward path for an obvious return to the car park.

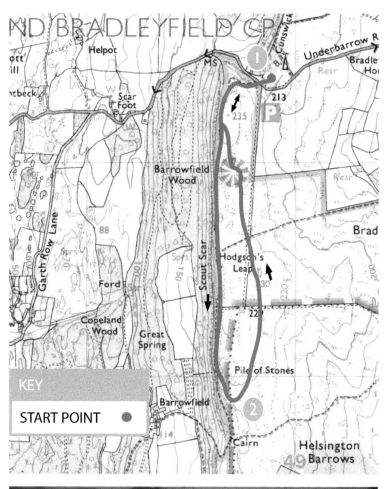

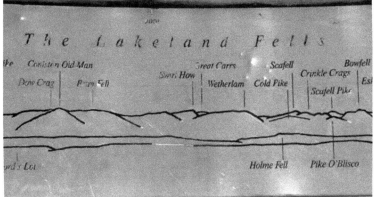

SHAP & SHAP ABBEY

THIS IS AN UNDEMANDING CIRCUIT ACROSS UPLAND FARMING
COUNTRY LINKING THE VILLAGE OF SHAP WITH THE PRIMITIVE
CHAPEL AT KELD AND THE RUINS OF SHAP ABBEY.

Shap is very much a linear village strung along the A6 Kendal to Penrith road. Prior to the construction of the M6 motorway, it was a busy place, its inns and shops providing for the needs of the many travellers using this great highway to and from Scotland.

From the mid 19th century the name 'Shap' has been universally known in railway circles as it was applied to the steep and lengthy inclines leading to the English summit of the main Euston to Glasgow line, although the actual summit is a few miles south of the village. Although the railway line provides the eastern boundary of the village, it is now a comparatively quiet place. In open country, at an altitude of nearly 900 feet (275 metres), it is frequently cold and windswept.

Shap Abbey of St Mary was founded early in the 13th century by the Premonstratensian or 'White Canons' Order, and was home to perhaps 12 or so of these brethren who ministered in surrounding parishes in addition to their monastic duties. Careful study of the ruins reveals various phases of the construction, with the 15th-century tower as the only substantial surviving part. Land holdings, both locally and further afield throughout Westmorland, were considerable. Dissolution came in 1540, since which date the structure has declined steadily, part being absorbed into a farm. It is now in the care of English Heritage and is open to the public without charge.

Keld chapel is probably of the late 15th century and is an interesting example of an unrestored pre-Reformation ecclesiastical building, with many original features including four of the five windows. The east window is similar to a window in the tower of Shap Abbey. The chapel was used for some years as a cottage, hence the fireplace, chimney breast and chimney. The roof is modern, following the collapse of the original some years ago. The simply furnished chapel has been in the care of the National Trust for many years and is open to visitors. The key is kept at a nearby house (notice on chapel door). The chapel remains consecrated, a service being held in August each year.

Not very much remains of the avenue of stones generally known as Shap Avenue. Over the centuries the railway builders and local farmers have shown little respect for this late Neolithic/early Bronze Age monument. Most obvious is the Goggleby Stone, re-erected in a concrete box after a fall in modern times, but some others can also be seen.

THE BASICS

Distance: 3¼ miles / 5km

Gradient: Mainly on the level but a steep ascent near the Abbey

Severity: Easy/moderate

Approx time to walk: 1½ to 2 hours

Stiles: Nine (some awkward)

Map: OS Explorer OL5, The English Lakes, North-eastern area

Path description: A mixture of footpaths and lanes

Start Point: Car park in Shap village (GR NY 564151)

Parking: Small free car park with public conveniences on east side of main road in Shap village. Adjacent to Memorial Park (CA10 3NR)

Dog friendly: On leads for preference

Public Toilets: At car park

Nearest food: Pubs and cafe in Shap village

1. From the car park turn left along the main road for a little more than 100 yards (90m).

2. Turn right at a public footpath sign to go through a farm gate. Angle left in 20 yards (18m) through another gate, with a waymark. A not very distinct path over short grass keeps close to the limestone wall on the right. One or two of the stones of Shap Avenue may be seen. Go over a stile and bear right along an obvious path. In the middle of the meadow, as the path bends to the right, turn left along a lesser path leading to a stile over the wall. Go over two more stiles within a short distance, then a third to reach an old unsurfaced lane. Turn left towards farm buildings. A hundred yards (90m) short of the buildings

turn right into a similar lane. This is wide open rough upland farming country with just a few improved pastures showing a brighter green colour. In view ahead are the flanks of the hills and mountains around Swindale and Haweswater. Go through a farm gate and descend gently towards Thornship, a sizeable farmstead. After a right bend the way past the farm is obvious, joining the surfaced access road.

3. Continue to Keld hamlet. The primitive chapel is in the angle at the road junction. From the chapel go uphill along the road for less than 100 yards (90m). Turn left over a cattle grid at a signpost 'Footpath. Shap Abbey' and go along the upper edge of the garden of a newish house. Go over a stile and continue along the edge of a rough meadow. At a junction of paths at the end of the wall keep straight on. Climb over the wall on the left at a high and rather awkward stile, turning right to continue the same line to a stile over the wall ahead. The route, which is not well defined, is now just above a narrow strip of woodland with the River Lowther below. The Abbey suddenly comes into view. After a stile/gate turn left down a steep bank, rough underfoot or carry on a little further to the surfaced road serving the Abbey and turn sharp left. In either case cross the bridge to reach the Abbey.

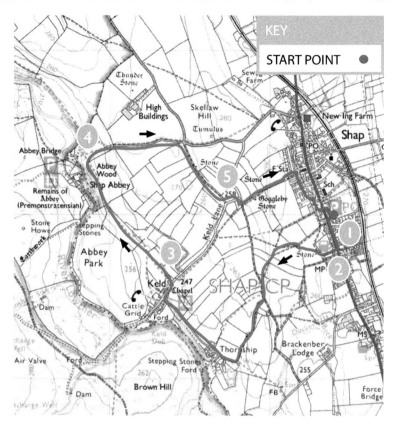

4. From the Abbey take the surfaced access road to climb quite steeply up the valley side to a cattle grid with a stile beside. Here a choice may be made between continuing along the very quiet road or going over the stile to follow a right of way along the edge of the field. The routes stay close together and end at the same place. Join the public highway and turn right at once into a narrow lane signposted 'Keld Lane'. There may be some obstruction of this lane but carry on regardless. Shap village is visible.

5. Turn left at the public road (Keld Lane) and in 100 yards (90m), turn right into another unsurfaced lane. Turn left in 40 yards (36m) over a waymarked stile. Ahead is the Goggleby Stone; another of the ancient stones can be seen on the left, close to a wall. The path back to Shap is now very clear: go along the field edge, over two stiles, up a small rise and head straight for the church. Go through a gate into the built-up area. Turn right along a back lane and then left to the main road. Turn right to return to the car park.

ST BEES

A CIRCUIT FULL OF INTEREST, INCLUDING HISTORIC ST BEES VILLAGE AND A LENGTH OF ATTRACTIVE COAST. YOU CAN RETURN EITHER ALONG THE CUMBRIA COAST PATH OR ACROSS THE BACK OF THE EXTENSIVE BEACH, WALKING ON SHINGLE AND SAND.

For the more energetic there is an alternative walk, following the Cumbria Coastal Path to the north, over one or both of the St Bees Head cliffs, with Fleswick Bay between the two. There are nature reserves and the cliffs have great populations of sea birds.

St Bees is, without doubt, one of the most interesting places on Cumbria's extensive coastline. In legend it was the landing place of St Bega, a young Irishwoman from a noble family who fled across the Irish Sea in a tiny, coracle-like boat, devoting herself to a life of great piety. Melvyn Bragg's novel Credo builds on the story, which also involves St Bega's Church by the side of Bassenthwaite Lake (see Mirehouse Walk, page 52).

The former priory, now the parish church , was founded in 1120 on an ancient religious site when Benedictine monks from York took over an existing church which they rebuilt during the latter part of the 12th century. The shaft of a Viking cross in the churchyard is evidence of earlier religious activity. The west door has a magnificent Norman arch and the church interior is very attractive, with a display of the 20th-century discovery of 'St Bees Man'. Throughout much of the 19th century a training college for Anglican clergy occupied the site. Across the road from the priory, St Bees School is a well-known and long established (1593) public school.

The Furness Railway, connecting Barrow with Carlisle, came to St Bees in 1849. The 'Coast to Coast' long-distance footpath established many years ago by the legendary Alfred Wainwright commences (or finishes!) at St Bees.

THE WALK

1.   Leave the car park along the access road; there is a wide roadside footpath.

2.   As the road forks, bear right. Turn left through a little gate in a few yards to follow a well-defined path, heading generally towards the priory church. After another gate, the Priory Paddock Wild Flower Garden is on the left. Continue, to join a road.

3.   The route goes to the right here, but a diversion of a few yards to the left is necessary

THE BASICS

Distance: 2¾ miles / 4.25km

Gradient: Level apart from main street in St Bees (and one significant ascent if route using Coastal Path is chosen)

Severity: Easy (or moderate if Coastal Path route is taken)

Approx time to walk: 1½ hours

Stiles: One (easy)

Map: OS Explorer 303, Whitehaven and Workington

Path description: Quiet roadsides and good paths

Start Point: St Bees beach car park (GR NX 961118)

Parking: Large car park behind St Bees beach (CA27 0EY)

Dog friendly: On leads for preference

Public Toilets: At car park

Nearest food: Beach café, Seacote Hotel and other pubs and cafes in St Bees

to visit the priory, with the entrance at the far (west) end. Back on course, walk by the roadside towards the railway level crossing, with station and signal box adjacent. Cross a bridge over a stream. Before the level crossing, at a road junction, a war memorial is on the right. Go a few yards along the minor road to discover a lovely statue of St Bega with her little boat. Cross the railway and continue along the attractive main street, rising gently. There is a good array of old stone houses, with village shop and inns, including the Coast to Coast bar at the Manor House. One unusual feature of the street was the former presence of several farms, of which only one now appears to be active.

4. After passing Fairladies Farm turn right at Seamill Lane, descending gently on tarmac. Look carefully for a footpath on the right; the signpost is behind a dense hedge. Follow this path as it descends to a kissing gate, cross the railway line, descend a few steps, go through another gate, cross a stream on a footbridge and continue over grass with a fence close on the left.

The Legend of ST BEGA

St Bega was the daughter of an Irish king, living some time between 600 and 900 AD. She refused to marry the man of her father's choice and fled in a small boat. Washed up here, she lived alone as a hermit, caring for the local people. When she moved on to an unknown destination, she left behind her arm-ring.

Although it is not even certain that Bega existed, the village was named after her, first as Kirkby Becoc, later St Bees. The monks of the Priory, founded here after 1120, were the custodians of a bracelet or arm-ring, believed to be her relic and they told her story. The ring remained here until 1539 when the Priory was dissolved.

After 1539, a garbled version of the legend became current, including this story. When Bega landed, she wanted to found a nunnery. She approached the Lord of Egremont, who laughingly promised her as much land as the snow would cover the next day. The next day was Midsummer Day. But it snowed!

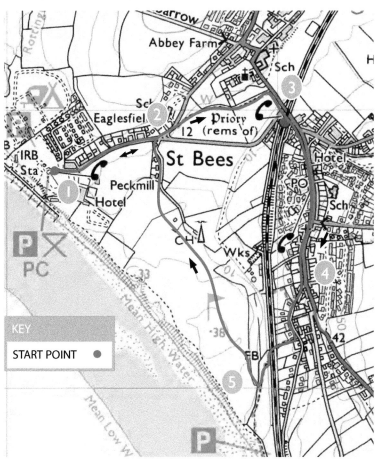

KEY

START POINT ●

5. Go over a signposted stile to join the Cumbria Coastal Path. Turn right and decide whether to follow the path rising above the sea cliffs (with a suitable warning notice) or to walk over shingle and/or sand. The state of the tide might well influence this decision! In either case return to the car park.

TARN HOWS

THIS BROAD, EASY TRACK AROUND A DELIGHTFUL SMALL
LAKE IS ARGUABLY THE MOST POPULAR WALK IN LAKELAND.

Largely man-made but very attractive gentle
Lakeland scenery surrounds the tarn, resulting
from the damming of a marshy valley to provide
power for a sawmill.

There were previously three smaller tarns. The
tree plantations have matured well to provide a
perfect setting for the tarn.

THE BASICS

Distance: 2 miles / 3km

Gradient: Level path around a small lake

Severity: Easy

Approx time to walk: 1 hour

Stiles: None

Map: OS Explorer OL7, The English Lakes, South-Eastern area

Path description: A broad, easy track around a delightful small lake

Start Point: National Trust car park at Tarn Hows (GR SD 326995)

Parking: National Trust car park (LA21 8DP). The access road to Tarn Hows leaves the Hawkshead to Coniston road close to Hawkshead Hill hamlet.

Dog friendly: On leads for preference

Public Toilets: At car park

Nearest food: Only an ice cream van at the car park, but there are pubs and cafes in Coniston and Hawkshead

TARN HOWS WALK

1. Leave the car park by the pedestrian access with vehicular barrier, cross the road, passing another vehicular barrier to follow a broad, easy, track towards the tarn. There are several junctions; stay with the main track descending steadily.

2. Go through a gate and cross the outlet stream. The track continues through the woodland by the shore of the tarn, crossing another stream. Keep right at a fork with a signpost before rising fairly steeply. Pass wayside seats; at a junction with signpost follow 'Hawkshead around tarn'.

3. Go through a gate to reach the head of the tarn and a little bridge. Black Crag is visible to the left. Continue, rising steadily at a gentle gradient. At the next junction go straight ahead for 'Coniston Yewdale', soon across open hillside, with lovely views of the tarn and its islands and with attractive picnic/play areas. Cross a stream, go through a gate and rise towards the public road, keeping left at a fork. Turn right at the road to return to the car park.

Shutterstock / Phil MacD Photography

Shutterstock / David Young

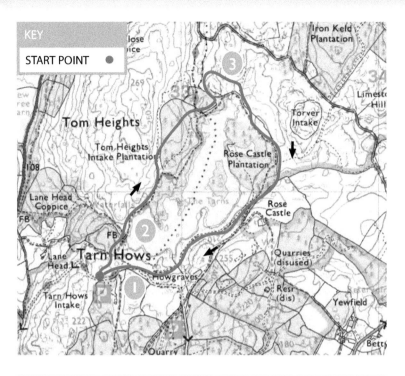

Shutterstock / Phil MacD Photography

WASDALE HEAD

THIS IS AN EASY LEVEL WALK AT THE FOOT OF SOME OF LAKELAND'S GREATEST MOUNTAINS. THE TINY FARMING COMMUNITY OF WASDALE HEAD SITS TIGHTLY BELOW THE MAJESTY OF GREAT GABLE, THE SCAFELLS AND OTHER FINE MOUNTAINS, ARGUABLY THE FINEST VALLEY HEAD IN THE COUNTRY.

The Wasdale Head Inn was the birthplace of British mountaineering, a meeting place for many of the finest 19th-century climbers who went on to pioneer the first ascents of many alpine peaks. The first landlord, Will Ritson, famous as the self-acclaimed world's greatest liar, has given his name to the bar which is part of the inn.

The graves of several climbers who were unsuccessful in meeting the challenges posed by the nearby mountains can be found in the graveyard of Wasdale Church, which is a candidate for the distinction of being Britain's smallest. A lovely little packhorse bridge behind the inn reminds us that for centuries trade routes reached Wasdale via the Black Sail and Styhead passes.

THE BASICS

Distance: 3 miles / 5km

Gradient: Level

Severity: Easy

Approx min time to walk: 1½ hours

Stiles: None

Map: OS Explorer OL6, The English Lakes, South-western area

Path description: Good tracks and a short length of minor road. Easy stepping stones.

Start Point: National Trust car park at Wasdale Head (GR NY 183076)

Parking: National Trust pay and display (members free) car park close to the National Trust camp site, (CA20 1EX). (It is not well signposted – turn right from the valley road at the first opportunity after passing the lake, cross a modern bridge and pass the entrance to the campsite)

Dog friendly: On leads for preference

Public Toilets: Toilets near car park and at Wasdale Head Inn

Nearest food: Ritson's Bar at the Wasdale Head Inn

WASDALE HEAD WALK

1. From the far end of the car park continue along the vehicular roadway.

2. Turn left before the bridge over Lingmell Gill, through a farm gate. In a few yards turn left again, through a kissing gate. Bear right to follow an unsurfaced roadway along the edge of the camp site to a gate/stile at the far end. There are waymarks along the way. Continue, crossing a stream on stepping stones, to join the valley road at a gate/stile. Walk along the roadside for a little more than 100 yards (100 m), passing public convenience and a sizeable parking area.

3. Fork right, along a public bridleway heading for the Styhead Pass, reaching the church in less than a quarter-mile (0.5 km). Continue to Burnthwaite Farm; the thick field walls and clearance piles are evidence of the efforts made in previous centuries to provide viable farming land in this inhospitable area.

4. Leave the Styhead route by turning sharp left at the farm. The path crosses and re-crosses a small beck before joining the major track descending from the Black Sail Pass.

5. Turn left to follow this track to the packhorse bridge behind the Inn. After any refreshment, cross the bridge, turning left to take a grassy track, keeping close to Mosedale Beck. Rejoin the valley road through a kissing gate, close to Down in the Dale bridge.

6. Turn right to walk by the roadside as far as the left turn and modern bridge to return to the car park.

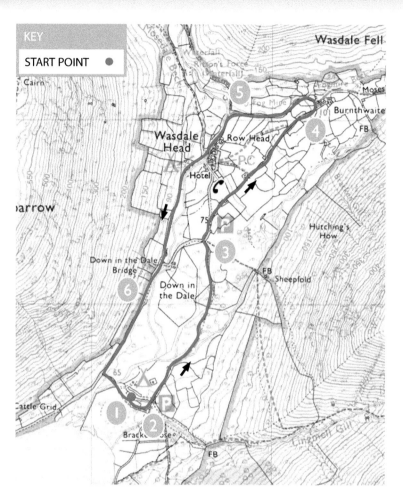

KEY

START POINT ●

SKINBURNESS

GRUNE POINT IS A FLAT, GENTLE, PROJECTION INTO THE WIDE EXPANSE OF THE SOLWAY FIRTH. ADJACENT ARE THE SOLWAY MARSHES WITH GRUNE POINT NATURE RESERVE, RICH IN BIRD LIFE.

Gorse is the predominant vegetation, with grazing land along the middle of the peninsula. The Point is the site of a Roman fort. Views include the Scottish coast, approximately six miles distant.

Apparently a small market town destroyed by a great storm several centuries ago, Skinburness has become a backwater hamlet, just a few houses and a derelict hotel. behind the inn reminds us that for centuries trade routes reached Wasdale via the Black Sail and Styhead passes.

THE BASICS

Distance: 3 miles / 4km

Gradient: Flat, Gentle

Severity: Easy

Approx time to walk: 2 hours

Stiles: None

Map: Ordnance Survey Explorer 314, Solway Firth, 1:25,000

Path description: Good walking surfaces. Approximately 200 yards of beach shingle

Start Point: Unmade road adjacent to Skinburness Creek, just off Skinburness Road (GR NY 129560)

Parking: No official car park. Places on verge of unmade road after passing the derelict hotel in Skinburness, a short distance to the north of Silloth

Dog friendly: On leads for preference

Public Toilets: None

Nearest food: None

SKINBURNESS WALK

1. Start along the unmade road, with a row of houses to the left, passing 'footpath' signposts but keeping straight ahead. At an apparent fork continue ahead. There are two kissing gates and the track is along the back of a beach. Pass a marker post (a left turn here results in a shorter walk).

2. Reach a stone construction almost concealed by gorse (this is probably the marker for the point). Although the land continues a little further, the recommended start for the return is to turn left immediately before the structure. The path is a little faint initially but soon becomes more pronounced, heading back towards Skinburness. There are occasional marker posts before the route becomes a little vague across a large grassy open area. Aim for a gate in the far right corner.

3. After the gate pass through an area of dense gorse, bearing right at an apparent junction. Cross another grass area as the track angles right to a shingle beach. In 200 yards rise to leave the beach, soon joining a public road at a gate.

4. Turn left, passing Chichester Hall. This is Dick Trod Lane. At a road junction turn left to pass the derelict hotel and return to the parking place.

© Ian Howe

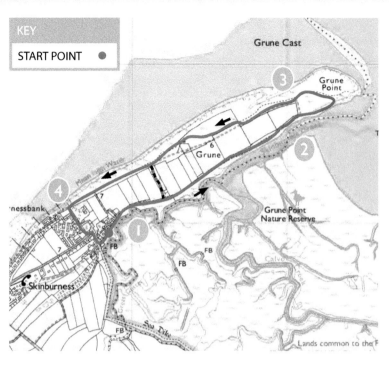

ABOUT THE AUTHOR

Following a professional career in environmental health, in partnership with his wife, June, Norman Buckley commenced writing guide books, mainly but not entirely footpath guide, in the early 1990's.

Almost forty books have so far been published, covering areas in the United Kingdom and Western Europe. A speciality has been the popular 'Level Walks' series. Over much of the same period, Norman and June have worked as walking consultants for a major holiday organisation.

Revelevant interests include photography, travel, railways and industrial archaeology Norman holds a Diploma in Environmental Management (Liverpool University) and a Master of Arts Degree in Lake District Studies (Lancaster University). The author is a member of the Guild of Outdoor Writers and Photographers.

Norman and June have lived in the Lake District since 1990.